D0459713

MIND-STRETCHING BRAIN FOOD

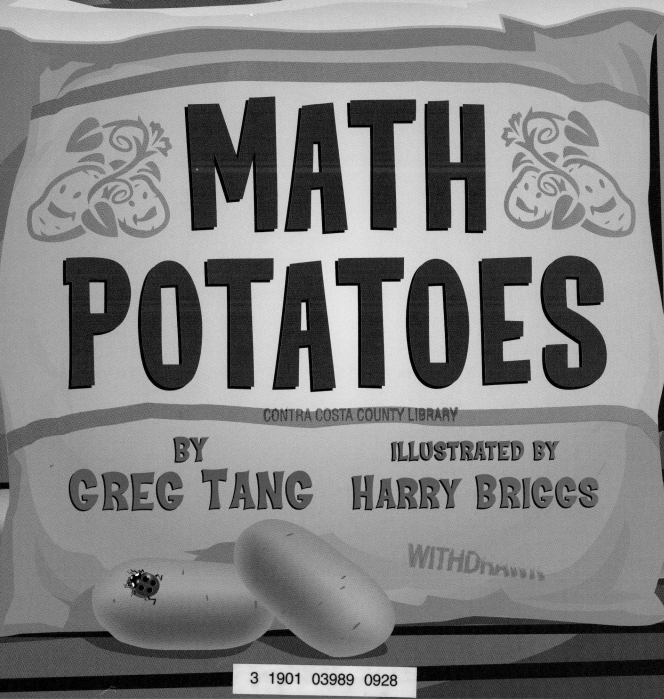

MATH POTATOES

BY
GREG TANG

ILLUSTRATED BY
HARRY BRIGGS

SCHOLASTIC PRESS • NEW YORK

A NOTE ABOUT *MATH POTATOES*

People often ask me, "Why did you start writing books?" The answer is simple. I wanted to make math easier for kids. When I looked around, so many kids were doing math the hard way. They were counting when they could be adding, they were adding when they could be multiplying, and they were memorizing when they could be understanding. No wonder they thought math was hard!

I believe math can and should be easy. My goal in writing *Math Potatoes* is to help kids ages 7–12 learn a few common sense strategies that make arithmetic faster and easier. In each problem, I intentionally present numbers in deceptive ways, using visual tricks based on color, spacing, and alignment to make less efficient groupings more obvious, and more efficient groupings less obvious. The idea is to challenge kids to combine numbers in smart ways, not just obvious ways.

I focus on three strategies in particular. The first is to make smart sums. Numbers like 10 and 15 are easy to work with, so it helps to look for them whenever possible. The second strategy is to find patterns and symmetries. Repeating groups simplify problems and make them easier to solve. The third strategy is to look for groups of equal size. Equal-sized groups make it possible to multiply instead of add, which is faster and leads to fewer mistakes.

Math Potatoes is the seventh book in a series that includes *The Grapes of Math, Math for All Seasons, The Best of Times, Math Appeal, Math-terpieces,* and *Math Fables.* Like the others, it combines math with poems and pictures to communicate in both verbal and visual ways. I hope all my books encourage kids to seek smarter, easier solutions, and I hope *Math Potatoes* provides healthy food for thought to kids everywhere. Bon appétit!

Greg Tang

www.gregtang.com

With love to Emily,
from your proud dad
—G. T.

To Lulu and Adrian
—H. B.

MATH-TER CARDS

Texas Hold 'em, 5-Card Draw,
7-Card Stud, and Omaha!

The trick is knowing when to hold,
When to raise and when to fold.

Can you add up every card?
The problem isn't very hard.

A straight, a flush, a pair of 3's —
Try one of each and it's a breeze!

SOCK HOP

At the dance the socks all mingle,
Most are paired, but some are single.

They do their best to keep the beat,
Please excuse the two left feet!

How many socks are hanging out?
Watch them as they twist and shout.

Look around for groups of 5,
Then get set to jump and jive!

HOME   VISITORS

TIME

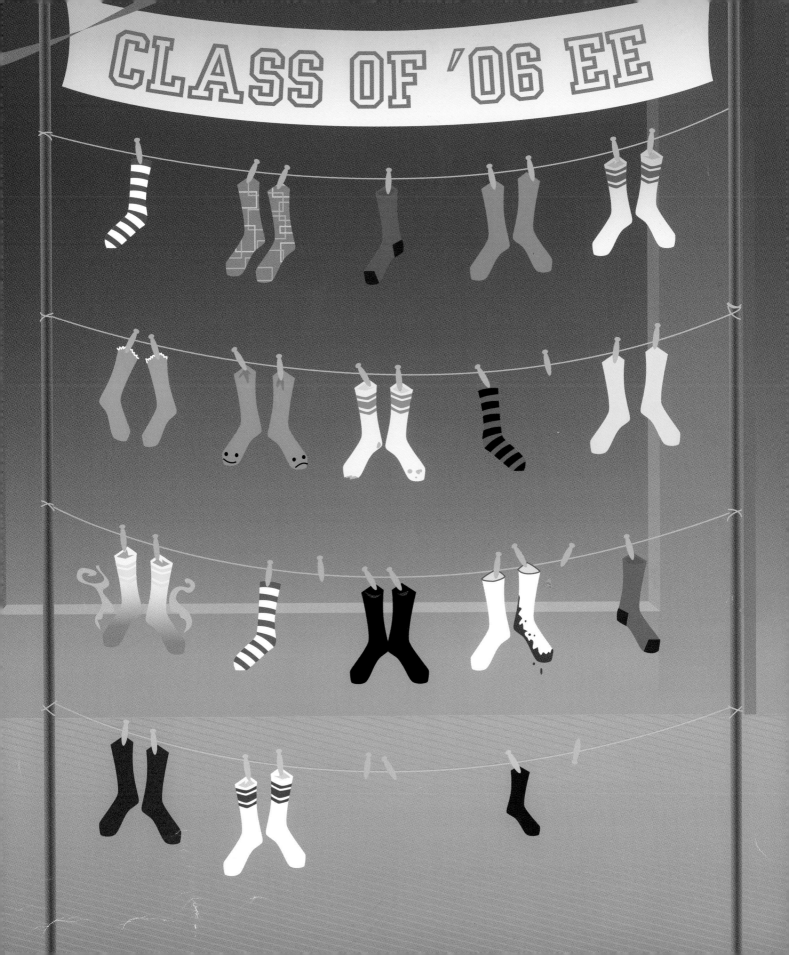

VEGETA-BULLIES

A squash will squash you on the ground,
And beets will beat you up and down.

But onions poke you in the eye —
They're the ones that make you cry!

Can you count the bullies here?
There's a fast way, have no fear.

In every group imagine 3,
Then subtract what you can't see.

SHELL SHOCK

I've never understood too well,
How oceans fit inside a shell.

Hold a conch up to your ear —
Crashing waves are what you hear!

How many shells have washed ashore?
Find a smart way to keep score.

Squares will yield the right amount,
As long as you don't double-count.

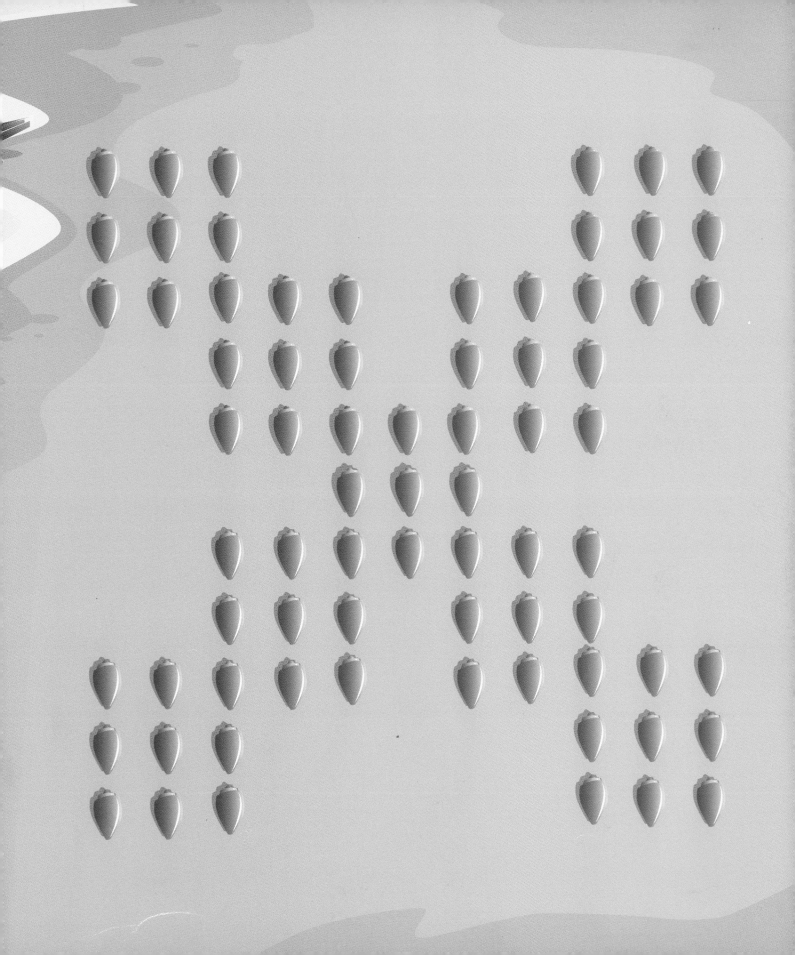

FOR SEVEN'S SAKE

I gaze into the evening sky,
Think great thoughts and wonder why.

Planets, stars, the Milky Way —
A window into yesterday.

Can you count each shining star?
The answer isn't very far.

When you look up to the heavens,
Try to think in groups of sevens!

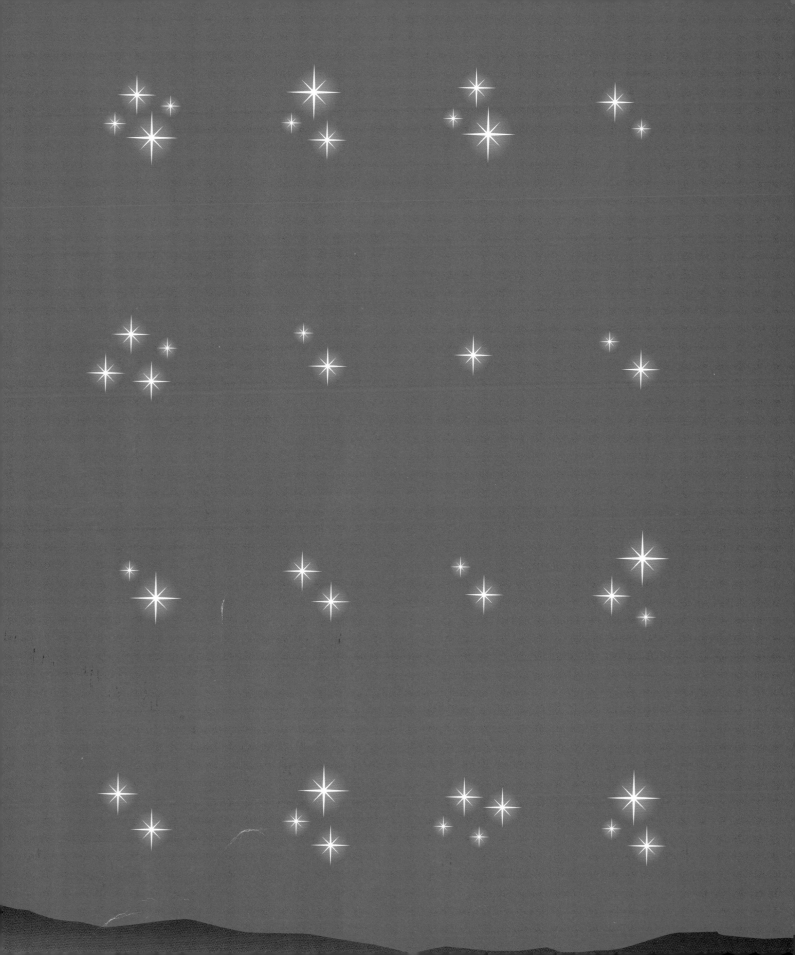

NUT HOUSE

Roasted dry and warm inside,
In their shell, the peanuts hide.

A little crack, a ray of light —
Now they're out in open sight!

How many peanuts in this snack?
Try to find a clever tack.

Don't just add what's right below,
Find smart ways to pair each row.

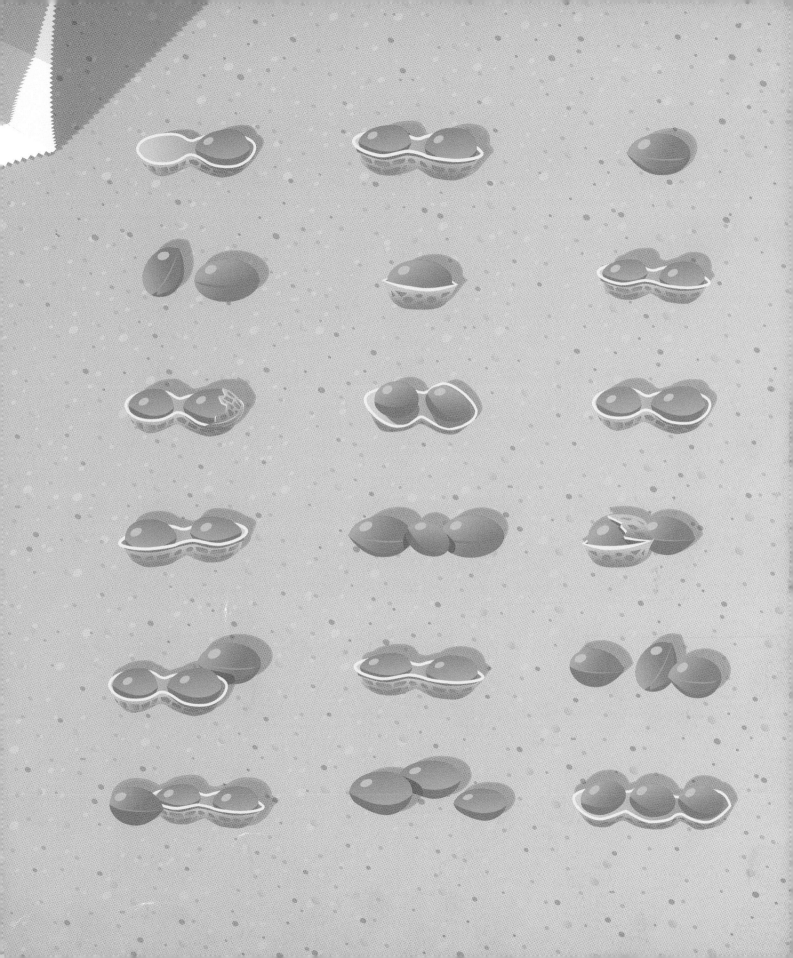

HANGING BY A THREAD

Oh, what tangled webs we weave,
When flies and bugs we do deceive.

Our silken threads will soon ensnare —
Unknowing victims in the air!

How many spiders lay in wait?
Cold and cruel is Nature's fate,

Think subtraction and you'll be,
Free from all this treachery!

SMART COOKIES

They start as bumpy lumps of dough,
Then in the oven heat they go.

Soon they are the perfect treat —
Food for thought that's good to eat!

Can you count each chocolate chip?
Here's a little, helpful tip.

Find the square in front of you,
Add the rest with place value!

PERFECT COOKIES
JXJ-2.0
4 CHIPS
VERSION 12.03
3.9

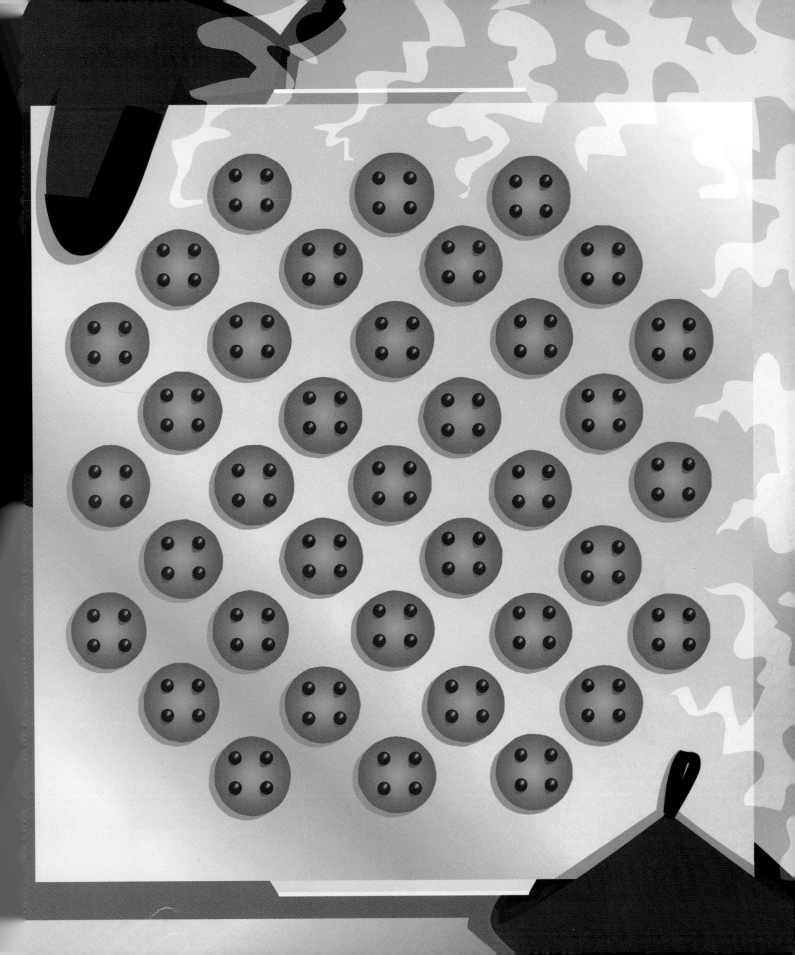

ONE-HIT WONDER

I'd like to be a concert star,
But need more in my repertoire.

I only know a single song —
And "Chopsticks" isn't very long!

How many notes are on this sheet?
Think smart and you won't miss a beat.

Instead of adding row by row,
Columns are the way to go!

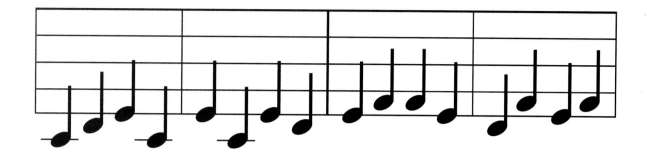

MATH POTATOES

Boiled and baked and often mashed,
Peeled and fried and sometimes hashed.

No wonder spuds hide underground —
Life is painful when they're found!

Can you add up these poor souls,
For whom the bell already tolls?

In groups of ten you'll hear their cries,
"Please don't turn us into fries!"

FLAT-JACKS

A breakfast food that's fun to make,
Short and round and called a cake.

Not the kind that stands up tall —
It's the flattest one of all!

How many pancakes can you eat?
Hurry now, but please be neat.

Rounding is a clever tact —
Just remember to subtract!

PEARLY WHITES

When buying pearls it's good to know,
The word in French for fake is "faux."

If smooth against your teeth they feel —
Then you know that they're not real.

How many pearls are on this strand?
So precious are these grains of sand.

Instead of counting every one,
Double three times and be done!

WAR OF THE ROSES

A dozen roses for my spouse,
Now she thinks I'm such a louse.

Her recent birthday I forgot,
Tonight I'm sleeping on a cot!

Can you count each long-stem rose?
Maybe they can cure my woes.

Don't add across or even down —
I hope forgiveness can be found!

THE EMPERORS' NEW CLOTHES

When it comes to formal wear,
Penguins are beyond compare.

Dressed up in a little tux,
They look like a million bucks!

How many penguins do you see?
Try to count them elegantly.

When you need to add in haste,
Equal groups are in good taste!

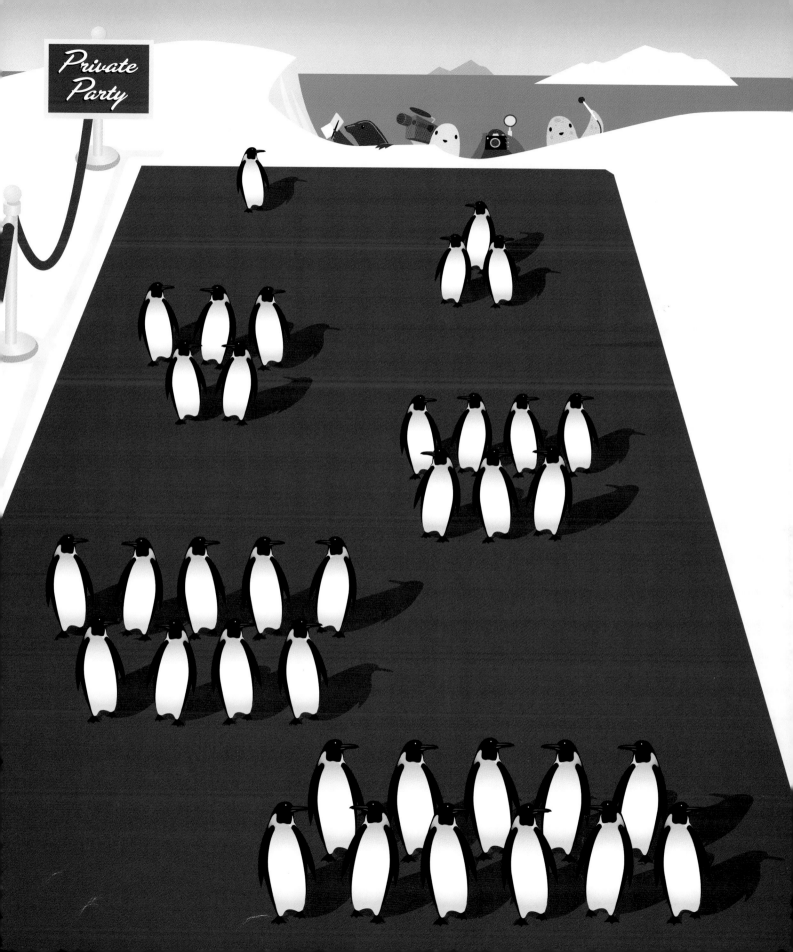

Private
Party

IN A PICKLE

If you're in a fickle mood,
Pickles are the perfect food.

Some are sour, some are sweet —
Either way, they're good to eat!

How many pickles in this bunch?
Try subtracting in a crunch.

Imagine eight in every row,
Just subtract and you will know.

CONE BEDS

Majestic pine trees touch the sky,
Raining cones from boughs up high.

A bed of needles makes a nest,
A soft and shady place to rest.

How many pinecones on the ground?
It helps to first move some around.

Simply fill in every gap —
Add them up and take a nap!

ANSWERS

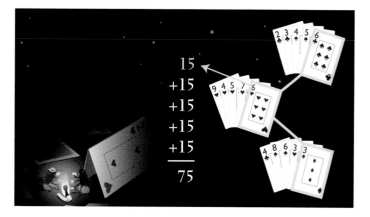

MATH-TER CARDS

Instead of adding all 5 cards in each hand, take one card from each and make groups of 3. The 5 groups each total 15, or 75 altogether.

$5\times15 = 15+15 + 15+15 + 15 = 75$

Alternatively, $5\times15 = $ half of $(10\times15) = 75$

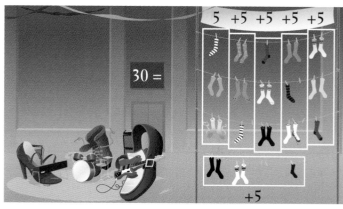

SOCK HOP

When possible, add numbers that have easy sums. The socks can be matched to create 6 groups that each total 5, or 30 socks altogether.

$6\times5 = 5+5+5 + 5+5+5 = 30$

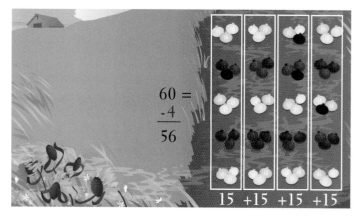

VEGETA-BULLIES

Imagine 4 additional onions so that each group has 3. There would be 15 (5×3) onions in each column and 60 (4×15) onions altogether. Subtract the 4 imaginary onions and you are left with 56 onions.

$(4\times15) - 4 = 60-4 = 56$

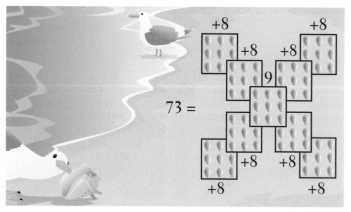

SHELL SHOCK

Start with the square in the middle that has 9 shells. Moving outward, find 8 squares with 8 new shells in each, or 64 (8×8) more shells. There are 73 shells altogether.

$9 + (8\times8) = 9+64 = 73$

FOR SEVEN'S SAKE

Instead of grouping by rows or columns, group by diagonals and make 6 groups of 7 stars, or 42 stars.

$6 \times 7 = 7+7+7 + 7+7+7 = 42$

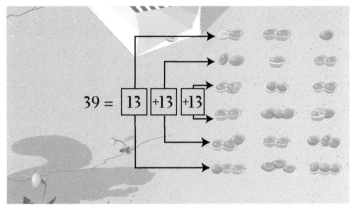

NUT HOUSE

When adding evenly spaced numbers, make groups of equal size by adding the first and last numbers, the second and second-to-last numbers, and so on. Here, the sum of each pair is 13, or 39 peanuts altogether.

$3 \times 13 = 13+13 + 13 = 39$

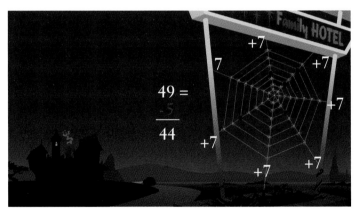

HANGING BY A THREAD

Imagine 5 spiders where they seem to be missing. There would be 7 strands of 7 spiders, or 49 spiders. Subtract the 5 imaginary spiders and you are left with 44 spiders.

$(7 \times 7) - 5 = 49 - 5 = 44$

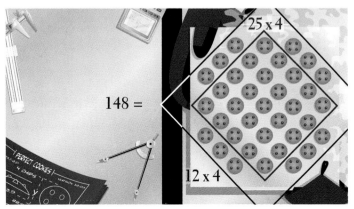

SMART COOKIES

Find a square with 5 rows of 5 cookies, or 25 cookies. Each cookie has 4 chips, or a total of 100 (25×4) chips. There are 12 (4×3) more cookies, which add another 48 (12×4) chips, or 148 chips altogether.

$(25 \times 4) + (12 \times 4) = 100 + 48 = 148$

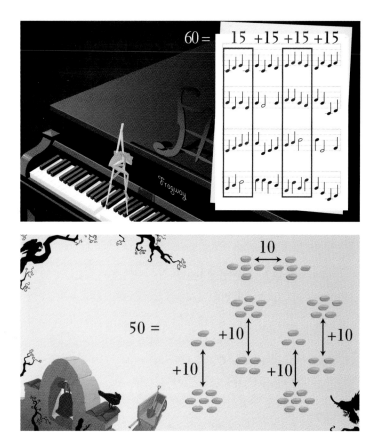

ONE-HIT WONDER

Instead of grouping by rows, group by columns and make 4 groups of 15 notes, or 60 notes.

$4 \times 15 = 15+15 + 15+15 = 60$

MATH POTATOES

When possible, add numbers that have easy sums. The potatoes can be paired to create 5 groups that each total 10, or 50 potatoes altogether.

$5 \times 10 = 10+10 + 10+10 + 10 = 50$

Alternatively, $5 \times 10 = $ half of $(10 \times 10) = 50$

FLAT-JACKS

Each column has 19 (5+4+3+4+3) pancakes. Round to 20 by imagining 1 more pancake in each column. There would be 4 columns of 20 pancakes, or 80 pancakes. Subtract the 4 imaginary pancakes and you are left with 76 pancakes.

$(4 \times 20) - 4 = 80 - 4 = 76$

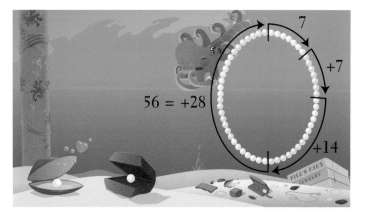

PEARLY WHITES

Use symmetry to see 8 groups of 7 pearls. To multiply by 8, double three times: 7 doubled once is 14, doubled twice is 28, doubled 3 times is 56.

$8 \times 7 = 7+7 + 7+7 + 7+7 + 7+7$

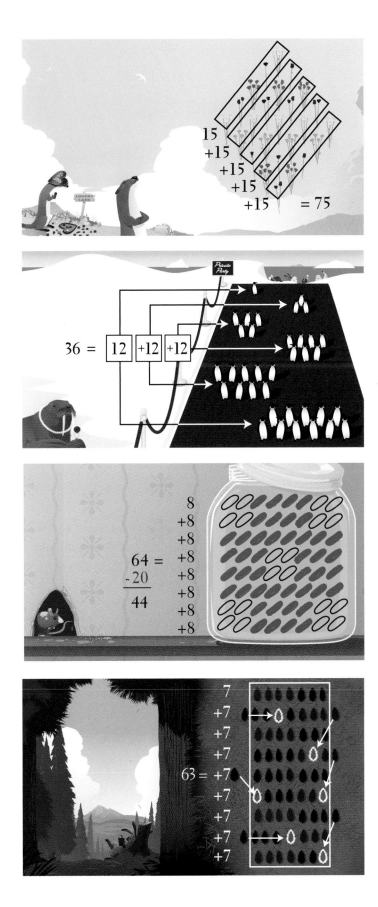

WAR OF THE ROSES

Instead of grouping by rows or columns, group by diagonals and make 5 groups of 15 roses, or 75 roses.

5x15 = 15+15 + 15+15 + 15 = 75

Alternatively, 5x15 = half of (10x15) = 75

THE EMPERORS' NEW CLOTHES

When adding evenly spaced numbers, make groups of equal size by adding the first and last numbers, the second and second-to-last numbers, and so on. Here, the sum of each pair is 12, or 36 penguins altogether.

3x12 = 12+12 + 12 = 36

IN A PICKLE

Imagine 4 pickles in each of the 5 squares where they seem to be missing. There would be 8 rows of 8 pickles, or 64 pickles. Subtract the 20 (5x4) imaginary pickles and you are left with 44 pickles.

(8x8) − (5x4) = 64−20 = 44

CONE BEDS

Move a pinecone into all the gaps where one is missing and make a rectangle with 9 rows of 7 pinecones. There are 63 pinecones altogether.

9x7 = 7+7+7 + 7+7+7 + 7+7+7 = 63

Alternatively, 9x7 = (10x7) − 7 = 63

ACKNOWLEDGMENTS

Special thanks to Harry Briggs, Liz Szabla, David Caplan,
Stephanie Luck, and Daniel Narahara

Library of Congress Cataloging-in-Publication Data
Tang, Greg.
Math potatoes: mind-stretching brain food / by Greg Tang;
illustrated by Harry Briggs.— 1st ed. p. cm.
1. Arithmetic—Juvenile literature. I. Briggs, Harry, ill. II. Title.
QA115.T3575 2005   793.74—dc22   2004016638
ISBN 0-439-44390-3
10 9 8 7 6 5 4 3 2 1   05 06 07 08 09

Printed in Singapore   46
First edition, July 2005
The text type was set in Electra LH Bold.
The display type was set in Coop Condensed.
Harry Briggs's artwork was created on the computer.
For more information about Greg Tang and his books,
visit www.gregtang.com. Book design by Greg Tang